Phil Moser can be summed up in two words. Biblical and p...
is a master at applying the Scriptures to everyday issues in such a way that people walk away with lives changed.

> KEVIN O'BRIAN
> Pastor, Ocean City Baptist Church

Phil Moser has done an admirable job of identifying spiritual principles and then applying them to daily life. I commend this work both to those struggling with their daily walk, and to those counselors who are seeking additional tools.

> DR. JOHN MACARTHUR
> Pastor-Teacher, Grace Community Church
> President, The Master's Seminary

Hats off to Phil Moser for helping us navigate through life's most challenging issues in a clearly biblical way. The thing I like about these booklets is that they are forged by a pastor who has successfully wrestled through these issues with his flock, and thankfully he now shares them with the church at large.

> DR. JOE STOWELL
> President, Cornerstone University

It has been a high privilege to know Phil Moser for more than 20 years. He is one of today's most gifted communicators; possessing an unusual ability to deliver biblical truth in an intensely personal and practical way. Our guests and students rate him a perennial favorite. I can give no higher recommendation for your next conference or speaking opportunity.

> DON LOUGH
> Executive Director, Word of Life Fellowship

Pastor Phil's writing reflects a deep commitment to helping individuals both understand and obey God's Word in their daily life. As an experienced counselor he realizes that just teaching the truth is not enough; people need help on the practical steps of disciplining themselves for the purpose of godliness. I commend this combination of exposition, call to obedience and "how-to."

RANDY PATTEN
Director of Training and Advancement
Association of Certified Biblical Counselors

As an educator, Phil Moser is distinctively gifted. His pedagogical skill enables him to clearly explain very difficult concepts in understandable language that all learners can grasp. Audiences would greatly benefit by his teaching.

CAROL A. SHARP, PH.D.
Served as Dean of the College of Education 2002-2012
Rowan University, Glassboro, New Jersey

I have been greatly encouraged by Phil's teaching. When I listen to him, I always walk away with more. More knowledge, more insight, more understanding, more hope. He's my go-to-guy when I have questions about the Bible or Christian living.

MICHAEL BOGGS
Singer-Songwriter
Winner of Multiple Dove Awards

The Biblical Strategies materials have been a big plus for our adult classes. With the inclusion of the memory verse packs and accountability study guides, the materials lend themselves readily to the discipleship process.

STEVE WILLOUGHBY
Pastor, First Baptist Church of Patchogue, New York

Safe in the Storm

biblical strategies for overcoming anxiety

Phil Moser

Safe in the Storm: biblical strategies for overcoming anxiety

Published by Biblical Strategies.
Distributed by Send the Light.

Visit our Web site: www.biblicalstrategies.com.

© 2013 Phil Moser
International Standard Book Number: ISBN: 978-0-9881942-5-0

All rights reserved. No part of this book may be reproduced without prior written permission from the publisher, except where noted in the text and in the case of brief quotations embodied in critical articles and reviews.

Credits:
Cover Art: gracewaymedia.com, Gary Lizzi
Cover Photograph: Elie Lighthouse in Scotland, Stuart Low
Copy Editors: Wes Brown, Justin Carlton

Contributions:
Thanks to Cindy Russell for "Key Passages & Psalms for the Anxious" (page 64), and Joe Schenke for "10 Truths to Combat the Deceiver's Lies" (page 66).

All Scripture quotations, unless otherwise indicated, are taken from THE HOLY BIBLE, English Standard Version. © 2001 Crossway Bibles, a ministry of Good News Publishers. Used by permission. All rights reserved.

CONTENTS

When the Storm Comes.................................5

Part 1: Think like God Thinks
    The First Principle: Belief
        Believe the Word, not your feelings 7
    The Second Principle: Change
        Change your mind, not your circumstances............15
    The Third Principle: Desire
        Desire God more than relief from your anxiety 35

Part 2: Do What Jesus Did
    Focus on the eternal 44
    Increase your dependence 46
    Review God's promises...........................48

Part 3: Follow as the Spirit Leads
    Avoiding *if only* and *what if* 51
    Practicing your new thoughts 56

Braving the Storm 58

Practical Suggestions

Prayer
    Prayer patterns & names of God 59

Bible Study
    Key Bible passages, & 28 daily Bible readings
        for overcoming anxiety...........................64

Scripture Retrieval
    Memorizing Scripture from defensive & offensive postures ..66

Holy Spirit Dependence
    Philippians 4:8 Stop sign, thought filters, triangle of
        God's character & 3 circles of clarification...........68

WHEN THE STORM COMES

BIG ROCK Candy Mountain loomed in the distance. I pulled the car off the dirt road and parked it, forgetting the way everything in Colorado appears closer than it really is. Ever since I'd spotted the massive stone a year ago, it had been my desire to hike to its base. I'm not a rock climber, but I do enjoy being awed by God's creation. And this rock could do it: a solid sheet of granite towering 1,400 feet above the South Platte River. That's only a hundred feet shy of the Empire State building. I shielded my eyes and tried to imagine New York City's tallest building standing next to the rock— it didn't seem possible.

For two and a half hours I hiked underneath a clear Colorado sky. But as I drew near the mountain, dark, ominous clouds appeared on the horizon. As I descended into the canyon, I felt the temperature falling. Nearing the river's edge, I heard the thunder echoing down the canyon's walls. Big Rock Candy Mountain towered with its skyscraper-like height on the opposite bank, but I didn't have time to study it. My eyes scanned the mountainside, looking for shelter. A small ponderosa pine leaned over an even smaller boulder about a hundred yards off. The rain started falling, and I was running by the time I reached safety. I slipped out of my backpack and slid under the tree, pressing my back against the small granite boulder. Lightning cracked on the opposite bank, and thunder reverberated off the granite walls. I stared in disbelief as the once lazy river was whipped to a frenzy. The wind drove the rain down in great sheets. But hidden by the rock, I looked on—safe in the storm.

From my hiding place, I could see the blue sky off to

the west as the wind drove the storm down though the canyon. The river settled down, the rain stopped, and the wind left behind a quiet coolness. I peaked out from beneath the branches and smiled at the irony. I had come to stand in awe of Big Rock Candy Mountain, but the most important rock in the canyon had been a six-foot boulder on the bank of the river. In the shadow of that rock I had found shelter.

Anxiety can feel like a storm. Threatening black clouds wipe out a blue sky. Your smile melts under the stress. You feel lost in the wilderness, and you can't outrun your anxious thoughts. This is not a book about how you can avoid a storm; rather, it's about how you can be safe in the midst of one.

You're not alone in your struggle. There are others who are frightened, too. Writing on anxiety has forced me to acknowledge my personal struggle with the issue. I can be a worrier. I often couch it in language like *I'm concerned* or *burdened*. Somehow that sounds better than *I'm worried and anxious*. My loving wife graciously reminds me that I am using the terms *worried* and *concerned* synonymously and that I shouldn't. She is right. Whether it is our financial future, the kid's productivity in school, or a situation looming at work, my mind can become consumed. I can easily obsess over areas outside of my control. When I do that, I am worrying. I am just unwilling to admit it.

While knowing that there are others who struggle may bring consolation, it doesn't necessarily bring comfort. For the comfort you desire, you will need to turn to the God who cares. In his wisdom, he has provided resources for your battle. The Father, the Son, and the Spirit stand ready to help you. Your part will be to think like God thinks, do what Jesus did, and follow as the Spirit leads.

THINK LIKE GOD THINKS
The First Principle: Belief
Believe the Word, not your feelings

AS LONG as Peter could remember he had worried about what others thought of him.[1] Silence, even in a crowd, had always felt awkward. So he would speak quickly and brashly, even if he later regretted what he had said. Most people thought it was his mouth that got Peter in trouble, but really it was his fear.[2] Peter knew this, even though he attempted to hide it from everyone else. But Peter knew that there was somebody else who knew too—Jesus. Jesus had discovered his struggle with fear on their first fishing excursion when every fish from the Sea of Galilee was trying to get in Peter's boat.[3] Every evil deed he'd ever done came rushing back to his memory. He buried his face in the boat full of fish, and pleaded with Jesus to leave.[4] When Jesus spoke, it was not what Peter expected. *Do not be afraid. From now on you will be catching men.*[5] Odd, Peter thought, that he would be chosen, for though he was courageous outwardly, he was afraid on the inside.

This wouldn't be Peter's final struggle with anxiety. Sometime later on that same lake, with a storm brewing, Jesus would speak to him again. *Take heart; it is I. Do not be afraid.*[6] While he attempted to be brave on his own—even trying to walk on water—he couldn't keep those anxious thoughts at bay.[7] Later, when he, along with James and John, were invited to the transfiguration of Jesus, Peter's anxiety rose again; this time to the point of terror. Before he knew it, he was prostrate on the ground again, unable to look at Jesus. And again, Jesus spoke. *Rise, and have no fear.*

Whenever Peter was anxious, his mouth would engage, even if his mind wouldn't. That's why, on the night of Jesus' betrayal, we find Peter speaking again to persuade the others that this time he wouldn't be afraid. All agreed his speech was convincing; this time they would be brave, too. But Peter's anxious thoughts about his future persisted. They swarmed over him. First he doubted, then he bailed. First he denied his relationship with Jesus to a 14-year-old girl, then to two others. Finally, he looked right into the eyes of Jesus[8] and did the very thing he swore he would never do. Peter had to learn that, when it comes to anxiety, you can't trust in yourself. You can't fake courage. Your only hope is to place your trust in God.

F IRST Peter 5:7 is one of the sweetest verses in the Bible. Peter recorded this truth for people who were under severe persecution. He writes, "Casting all you anxieties on him, because he cares for you." We all have the desire to control things that we cannot, and we often forget how deeply God cares for us. If I had authored the verse, I might have chosen a different quality of God to emphasize. Something like his perfect wisdom or his unlimited power. Logically, it would make more sense to think that even though I am not in control, an all-wise, all-powerful God is. But the Holy Spirit saw fit to inspire Peter otherwise, and I'm glad he did. When it comes to anxiety, he chose to emphasize the compassionate, softer side of God. When I am fearful, I find comfort in this truth: I'm not alone in my struggle, and God cares.

The challenge, of course, is that anxiety can wake you up at 3:00 AM. The silence in your house echoes the message: *No one's here and no one cares.* In these times we feel so very alone. We stare into the darkness trying to find a reasonable solution to the trouble we're in. The alarm clock interrupts our thoughts, but not our sleep, a shrill reminder that this is the time we should be waking up had our anxious thoughts not awakened us earlier. As we enter into the day, all those around us seem to interact quite naturally with one another. They laugh about their weekend. They complain because it's Monday. They tell stories about their relationships or listen to others who do. We smile and exchange formalities as if we're part of the group, but our anxious thoughts are all our own. They whisper deceitfully: *No one knows, and no one cares.* But the Bible tells us this is not entirely true. It may be true that the smiling people around you are clueless to your difficulty. It might even be true that some of them, if they knew, wouldn't care. But God knows, and he cares.[9] This is why the first principle of overcoming anxiety is *belief*. You and I must learn to believe God's Word, not our feelings.

We live in a world where feelings reign supreme. Listen attentively to the conversations around you, and I'm sure you'll agree. Every day, people are making life-changing decisions from a feelings-foundation. Statements like, *I feel like this is the best decision for me,* or *I just don't feel like I love him anymore* are commonplace. This mindset has even drifted into our spiritual conversations. I often hear people say *I feel like this is God's will for me* or *I just had a feeling that it was the right thing to do*. Because our feelings are personal, deeply felt, and sincere, they are easy to believe. But that doesn't mean that we should believe them. The root word for "believe" occurs 241 times in the New Testament. Nearly half of those times it is used by the apostle John. He directed us to believe the Father, his promises, his Word, and his Son. But not once did he say we should believe what we feel. This is the necessary starting point for victory over feelings of anxiety. It's time to ask yourself: *what do I really believe?*

Trust Him.
It may not feel like God cares, but he does.

Anxiety comes when I believe I have to carry the burden alone. My thoughts whisper to me: *Even those closest to you do not understand this like you do.* This is easy to believe because others don't appear to be as burdened by your very real circumstances. This presumption is evident in the disciples when they face a violent storm on the Sea of Galilee. Mark recounts the story:

> And a great windstorm arose, and the waves were breaking into the boat, so that the boat was already filling. But he was in the stern, asleep on the cushion. And they woke him and said to him, "Teacher, do you not care that we are perishing?"[10]

Notice how quickly the disciples went from fear to a perceived flaw in the character of Jesus. They wrongly assumed that if he cared he would do something to change their circumstances. When you're bailing water for all you're worth, it's easy to assume that God doesn't care about you. The Bible doesn't question the reality of the storms that come into your life. It doesn't call you weak because you're afraid. Instead, it tells us to do something with our worrisome thoughts and fear: cast them on the Lord.

The word "cast" is used elsewhere in the Bible to indicate the act of taking off an outer garment and throwing it to the ground. This is both descriptive and helpful. Just as there is a disconnect between the garment and wearer when he casts it to the ground, there is a similar relationship that occurs between the anxious thoughts and the worrier. Take your anxious thoughts and throw them at the feet of the God who cares. Obviously, such an action will require a great deal of trust in the Lord. *What if he doesn't do anything with them? What if he's too busy to concern himself with my problems? What if he doesn't care after all?* Perhaps this is why the compassionate side of God is emphasized in verse 7. We are to remember the concerned, caring side of God (you will find a list of the various names of God on page 63). When feelings of anxiety begin to rise in your chest, that is the time to rehearse the caring attributes of God. Remind yourself that he knows and cares. Trust him.

Humble Yourself
It may not feel like pride, but it is.

To properly interpret 1 Peter 5:7, allow your eye to wander to the verse before and after it.[11] Peter sets up the context of verse 7, with the thought that comes before it. In verse 6 he writes, "Humble yourselves, therefore, under the mighty hand of God so that at the proper time he may exalt you", then he adds verse 7, "casting all your anxieties on him, because he cares for you."[12] While it may come as a surprise, humility is an important part of overcoming anxiety. We worry about all kinds of stuff, like: job security, our kid's success, the dreaded doctor's call, or conflict among friends.

There is a common feature in most of the things we are anxious about: we can't control the outcome. When we are not walking in humility, we are susceptible to the false belief that if we think about it long enough we can control the outcome. When the situation is outside of your control, such a thought reveals a prideful spirit. You think you can do what only God can do. God is ultimately in control of all things.[13] You are not. That's why Peter warns us, "Humble yourself under the mighty hand of God." While ongoing anxious thoughts may not feel prideful, they are. The point of the context is this: if you are unwilling to humble yourself before God, you will be unable to cast your anxieties upon him.

Guard you thoughts.
Wrong thinking may not feel harmful, but it is.

In verse 8, Peter gives another warning: "*Be sober-minded; be watchful*. Your adversary the devil prowls around like a roaring lion, seeking someone to devour" [emphasis added].[14] The Greek word for sober-minded (some translate it self-controlled) occurs only four times in the New Testament. Each time it is in the context of suffering.[15] We should expect that when we face a trial it's going to be difficult to think clearly. The Greek word *nepho* (translated here as sober-minded) means to be free from the influence of intoxicants.[16] It comes from the word that means "to avoid drunkenness." In this context, it is a crucial reminder to see your battle with anxiety as a spiritual one. Be alert. Be vigilant. The devil is active and aggressive, like a hungry lion.

But there is another warning as well. Just like being under the influence of alcohol can impair your thinking, so can being under the influence of worry. Worry makes it hard to think in terms of biblical priorities.[17] Your anxious thoughts consume your thinking. Like an addiction, such thinking becomes difficult to break. That is why we're charged to be sober-minded. In order for an alcoholic to be victorious in his struggle, he must learn to say "no" to the next drink. The same is true of the anxious person. They must learn to say "no" to their worrisome thoughts. They must be watchful, aware of when a plan for the future morphs into worrying about it.

Our struggle with anxiety is ultimately a struggle of belief. Will we believe what our feelings are telling us or what God's Word is proclaiming? Being settled on this matter is the first step in the process of overcoming anxiety. But how do we change? That is the subject the next chapter. First, determine what you will believe, then read on.

The Second Principle: Change
Change your mind, not your circumstances

SOMETIMES the most profound statements come from the most ordinary circumstances. Years ago, I was helping my daughter, who was in 5th grade at the time, with her Math homework. The assignment was introducing her to the metric system. Suddenly, I had a flashback. There I was, sitting in my 5th grade classroom, and my Math teacher was telling us that we needed to learn the metric system because within a few years everyone in America would be using it. I shared the thought with my daughter, and added this comment: "Here we are 35 years later, and Americans are still stubbornly refusing to switch to the system that everyone else uses. I wonder why that is?" My eleven year old looked up from her homework as if the answer was obvious. She distilled 35 years of history into less than 20 words when she said, "People don't like change, dad. Well, unless of course they get something out of it for themselves."

You will never overcome anxiety without making fundamental changes in the way that you think. Some of these changes, you won't like much at first. They will seem too harsh, too basic, or too difficult. You will be prone to believe that what you really need is a change of circumstances. So you switch schools, jobs, and marriages, if necessary. But before long, you discover that the same patterns you had earlier with anxiety reoccur in your new surroundings. What you need is a change of mind, not a change of circumstances. This is why the Scripture says, "Do not be conformed to this world, but be transformed by the renewal of your mind, that by testing you may discern what is the will of God."[18]

Paul's letter to the Philippians carried some of the most practical advice for overcoming anxiety you will find anywhere. In Philippians 4:6-8 we discover that we will need to change how we think about worry, how we think about prayer, and what we think about.

Change how you think about worry.
God commands us not to worry; when we do, we sin.

More often than not, worry feels like something that happens to us. Like a bad case of the flu, we were simply going about our daily business, and it found us. Because worry is a way of thinking, it is natural for it to become your default response. For the repeat offender, for whom worry is their first response, it is easy for it to seem like worry is the culprit and not a choice.

When we face dangerous situations it is natural for us be afraid. Worry is what takes place when we allow those fears to continue even after the danger is no longer looming. Let me illustrate. Recently I was in a life-threatening car accident. Miraculously, I walked away uninjured, but certain elements from the accident lingered in my mind. For instance, every time I slid into the driver's seat I could still hear the crunch of the metal, feel the explosion of the air bags, and see the shattered windshield. Such thoughts, if left unattended, could become debilitating. If I gave into my anxieties, I might give up driving temporarily, or eventually give it up all together. To combat those feelings I would thank the Lord for sparing my life, set my mind on biblical truth, and then, by faith, start the car and pull out of the garage. It took a few weeks, but eventually those anxious thoughts were dispersed, driven from my memory by a renewed dependence on God. Feelings of anxiety are understandable when we're in imminent danger, but forbidden by the Scriptures when we are not.

Even though those anxious thoughts may feel like they control us, the Bible makes it clear they do not. Paul writes, "*Do not be anxious about anything*, but in everything by prayer and supplication with thanksgiving let your requests be made known to God" [emphasis added].[19]

The Greek language can, among other things, communicate the attitude of the writer in regards to the action. We call this the mood of the verb. It can be a declaration of fact,[20] a wish/possibility,[21] or a command.[22] When the Spirit of God communicated the action "do not be anxious" he emphasized the command. This is significant. Inherent in the command is that we have a choice to make: to obey or not obey, and to receive the subsequent consequences. If God had wanted to communicate that anxiety is an unchanging condition, he would have chosen the mood of *fact*. If he had wanted you to believe that overcoming worry was simply a desire, he would have used the mood of *possibility*. But God wanted you to realize that worry is a choice you make, so he used the *imperative* mood. He gave a command. Through the Spirit's power, you are both capable of obeying and expected to obey the command: *Do not be anxious*. In his book, *Respectable Sins*, Jerry Bridges has this to say about anxiety:

> When you or I say to someone, "Don't be anxious" or "Don't be afraid," we are simply trying to encourage the person, or admonish in a helpful way. But when Jesus (or Paul or Peter, who were writing under divine inspiration) says to us, "Don't be anxious," it has the

force of a moral command. In other words, it is the moral will of God that we not be anxious. Or to say it more explicitly, *anxiety is a sin.*

Anxiety is a sin for two reasons: First...anxiety is a distrust of God. In the Matthew 6:25-34 passage, Jesus said that if our heavenly Father takes care of the birds of the air and the lilies of the field, will he not much more take care of our temporal needs? And Peter told us that the basis of our casting of our anxieties on God is that He cares for us. So when I give way to anxiety, I am, in effect, believing that God does not care for me and that He will not take care of me in the particular circumstance that triggers my anxiety of the moment. [...] Anxiety is a sin also because it is a lack of acceptance of God's providence in our lives. God's providence may be simply defined as God's orchestrating all circumstances and events in His universe for His glory and the good of His people. Some believers have difficulty accepting the fact that God does in fact orchestrate all events and circumstances, and even those who do believe often lose sight of this glorious truth. Instead we tend to focus on the immediate cause of our anxiety rather than remembering that those immediate causes are under the sovereign control of God.[23]

While speaking about worry this way, may sound harsh, it is meant to help, not hurt. Thinking about anxiety as a choice grants you the freedom to overcome it. You are not a victim of your anxious thoughts. No matter how habitual they have become, they are choices that you make.

In my first booklet, *Just Like Jesus: Biblical Strategies for Growing Well*, I communicated the freedom that comes from considering your habitual thoughts in this way.

We often think of habits as the things that we do. Yet, few things become habits so quickly as the thoughts that we think. You probably do a number of "mindless" tasks to prepare to go to work or school in the morning. But are they really "mindless?" Or are they mental habits? Things like: brushing your teeth, taking a shower, pouring the cereal, and making the coffee. Our hurried culture even captures this truth. We say: "I never gave it a second thought." Are we not implying that we gave it a first thought?

This truth brings both good news and bad. The good news is that our thoughts are only habits, not involuntary actions. So, by the power of the Spirit, we can choose what we think about. There is hope for the destruction of old thought patterns and the development of new ones. The bad news is that because these thoughts come so quickly and frequently, they are challenging to break. This is why the Scripture says,

> You formerly walked according to the course of this world, according to the prince of the power of the air, of the spirit that is now working in the sons of disobedience. Among them we too all formerly lived in the lusts of our flesh, indulging the desires of the flesh and of the mind.

This biblical passage is an excellent reminder of the location of our battlefield. When we formerly lived in the lusts of the flesh, we indulged our desires and our minds. Walking in the Spirit means we develop a new set of thought patterns that help us control those sinful desires.[24]

Thinking about ongoing worry as sin does not mean that we will no longer struggle with it. Rather, God offers a solution when we try and fail. He is a forgiving God, and when we come to him with a repentant spirit, he forgives and offers grace in our time of need.[25] But confession alone isn't enough. God offers an additional resource for overcoming anxiety: prayer.

Change how you think about prayer.
Make it your pattern, not your panic button.

The Bible states, "Do not be anxious about anything, but in everything by prayer and supplication with thanksgiving let your requests be made known to God."[26] When I talk to someone struggling with anxiety, I usually start by asking questions about their prayer life. I have found that most people struggling with anxiety are praying, but their prayers tend to be one-dimensional: they're praying that God would take the anxiety away. For them, prayer is a panic button. They reach for it when the feelings become overwhelming. But praying this way doesn't have the staying power necessary to help us overcome anxiety. Fortunately for us, God didn't leave us uninformed. With over 650 prayers recorded in the Bible, we have examples for how to pray, whatever the situation.

I want to encourage you to think of prayer more as a pattern to develop than a panic button to push. The apostle Paul gives us one of these patterns immediately following his command to not be anxious. He writes,

> Do not be anxious about anything, but in everything by prayer and supplication with thanksgiving let your requests be made known to God. And the peace of God, which surpasses all understanding, will guard your hearts and your minds in Christ Jesus.[27]

For someone struggling with anxiety, this passage offers a

deeply sought after promise: *the peace of God...will guard your hearts and your minds in Christ Jesus.* But that promise is predicated upon a consistent prayer life, and Paul gives us four words that shape our conversation with God: prayer, supplication, thanksgiving, and requests.

Prayer: Realizing that Nothing is too Small or too Big for God.

The text tells us that we are to bring "everything in prayer." Nothing is too small for God to be concerned about. Jesus reminded us that his Father noticed when a sparrow fell from the sky.[28] There are an estimated 100 billion birds in the world. They come in all sorts and sizes, but God is aware of the loss of even the smallest. Don't think your cares are too little for God; he is interested in them. The Psalmist wrote that God's thoughts about the details of his life were vast. He said,

> Your eyes saw my unformed substance; in your book were written, every one of them, the days that were formed for me, when as yet there was none of them. How precious to me are your thoughts, O God! How vast is the sum of them! If I would count them, they are more than the sand.[29]

Because my family lives close to the Jersey Shore, during the summer we visit there frequently. The boardwalks, with their shops, rides, and places to eat, line the most popular beaches to the west; the Atlantic Ocean, with its thunderous waves, lies to the east. Because the shoreline isn't naturally protected, it is prone to erosion. Each year, they replenish the beaches with sand from the bottom of the ocean about a half a mile away, pumping it in huge pipes back up onto the beaches. And each winter, the ocean tears those beaches down, depositing that sand at the bottom of the ocean about a half a mile away. The project is massive; bulldozers and heavy equipment are required to reposition the sand once it's on the beach. The refurbishing of just one beach can cost 15 million dollars.[30] Ponder this: *God's thoughts about you are greater than all the sand on the seashore.* To correct an oft-used phrase, it's not the devil that's in the details—it's God.

For years, my wife Kym has brought the smallest of requests to the Lord in prayer. When we were first married, we moved to California so that I could attend seminary. Having only visited Los Angeles, I just assumed that finding housing would be a challenge. So I was delighted when a landlord called with a two bedroom apartment for the cost of a one bedroom. While we were only engaged at the time, I knew that Kym had been praying, so I couldn't wait to call her. I can still remember her words: "That's great, honey. Did you happen to ask if there was a laundry facility in the apartment complex? I had been praying specifically that there would be. Could you call the landlord back and ask him about it?" I remember thinking, "Are we going to let a little dirty laundry interfere with what is obviously an answer to prayer?" I hemmed and hawed trying to find a way to not bother the landlord with where we were going to wash our clothes. But Kym was so sweet about it (and persistent), that I made the call. It sounded something like this: "We're really thankful for the offer of the apartment, and we're ready to sign a lease, but my fiancé had been praying that there would be laundry facilities in the complex. Is there?"

"Yes, there is." Mr. Vickers replied. Then there was silence, as if he had more to say, but was trying to figure out how. "Phil, my tenants stay a long time. The one in your apartment had been there for 30 years. It's unusual for me to have an opening on such short notice. That's what makes your fiancé's prayer request special. The apartment that is open is the one next door to the laundry facility." We lived there for four years. During that time, the laundry facility was a constant reminder that no request is too small for God.

Jesus also taught that nothing was too difficult for God.[31] When we struggle with anxiety, we believe we must carry our difficulties—and their outcomes—alone. The Psalmist captured God's care and power together when he recorded,

> Of old you laid the foundation of the earth, and the heavens are the work of your hands. They will perish, but you will remain; they will all wear out like a garment. You will change them like a robe, and they will pass away, but you are the same, and your years have no end. The children of your servants shall dwell secure; their offspring shall be established before you.[32]

When our home was built, I watched as they poured the foundation. During excavation, they were careful not to disturb the soil where they would pour the concrete footers. In the years since our home was built, it hasn't shifted, in spite of the fact that it has been through two hurricanes. The secret is not the foundation of our home, it is the foundation of the earth. Because the earth beneath our home's foundation has remained undisturbed, our foundation has been secure. The same is true of our personal lives. Our God was not only powerful enough to lay the foundations of the earth, but with that same power he sovereignly directs the events of your life and mine. King Nebuchadnezzar acknowledged this when he said of God, "He does according to his will among the host of heaven and among the inhabitants of the earth; and none can stay his hand or say to him, 'what have you done?'"[33] For the God who laid the foundation of the earth and spun billions of stars into space, no task is too big. God is giving a pertinent reminder: through prayer, we bring our concerns to him. Think about your challenges differently. Don't think they're too small. God is interested. Don't think they're too big. God is able.

Supplication: Acknowledging Your Need to God.

The word "supplication" came to mean "pray," but that was not its original meaning. The root word *deesis* meant "to lack or to have need."[34] This is an important starting point for the person struggling with anxiety. We are prone to anxious thoughts because we try to carry burdens on our own, but we lack the strength or ability to sustain those burdens. This is why Peter encouraged us to "cast our burdens on the Lord."[35] We were not meant to carry them alone.

Most of us who battle anxiety rarely admit to others that it's a problem. Think about it: when was the last time you heard someone request prayer for their struggle with anxiety? You would think from the limited times it's mentioned at a prayer meeting, hardly anyone would struggle with it. But statistically that is not the case. One study declares that over 40 million Americans struggle with some form of anxiety.[36] While it is not unusual to request prayer for cancer or unemployment, it is the rare individual who will publicly acknowledge a struggle with worry and ask for others to pray for them. But this is exactly what God had in mind for our assistance. Don't be anxious, admit your need and bring it to the Lord.

On the night that Jesus was arrested and tried, he foresaw Peter's anxious heart and his unwillingness to admit it. Notice what he said:

> Simon, Simon, behold, Satan demanded to have you, that he might sift you like wheat, but I have prayed for you that your faith may not fail. And when you have turned again, strengthen your brothers.[37]

The word Jesus chose to use for "prayed" is the word translated in our Philippians 4:6 text as "supplication." Jesus is saying, *Peter, I see your lack. I recognize your need even if you refuse to admit it. I will pray for you.* A part of overcoming your anxiety is admitting your need. Bring it to God. Share it with others so that they can pray. Acknowledge your struggle, then continually pray for victory.

Thanksgiving: Looking for Reasons to Praise God.

The anxious person may initially struggle to find things for which to be thankful, but a thankful spirit is a habit that can be developed.[38] Paul mentions thanksgiving as the third step for prayer knowing that anxious thoughts cannot coexist with grateful ones. Deep in the anxious heart is the growing seed of discontentment. We believe that if only our circumstances would change we would be at peace. But peace, the very thing that we desire, remains elusive because we have tied it to circumstances that we can't control. The bottom line is we are discontent with our present situation. The practice of being thankful fosters a spirit of contentment even in the most dire of circumstances. Consider the biblical characters who were thankful in spite of the difficulties the faced: Job,[39] Jeremiah,[40] Paul.[41] Perhaps Paul stated it best:

> Not that I was ever in need, for I have learned how to

be content with whatever I have. I know how to live on almost nothing or with everything. I have learned the secret of living in every situation, whether it is with a full stomach or empty, with plenty or little. For I can do everything through Christ, who gives me strength.[42]

Paul doesn't see his circumstances as the cause of his thankful, contented Spirit. Rather, he sees those difficult times as opportunities to be grateful for the strength that Christ supplied that he might endure them. Elsewhere, he writes that the difficult times cause him to place his confidence in Christ and not in himself.[43] I once heard someone share, "God will not protect you from what he can perfect you through." This was the secret that Paul had discovered. God was increasing his spiritual endurance through the difficulties, and causing him to be more dependent on the Lord Jesus. This was the focus of Paul's gratitude. He was thankful for the opportunity to personally change; he was not looking to change his circumstances. This is a pattern of thinking that you can develop as well (see pages 68-73 for some practical ways you can apply this truth).

Requests: Seeking First the Kingdom of God.

Developing these first three steps of prayer will significantly change the content of your prayer requests. Your prayer time will feel less like hitting a panic button, and you will began to ask the Lord for better things than simply relief from your anxiety. Perhaps that is why Paul listed the "requests" as the final step of prayer. Imagine how your requests might change if you were careful to include these other three elements up front. Let's review those words and their applications together:

- Prayer: You start your prayer time with the understanding that no request is too small for God to be concerned with, nor is any request too large that God would be incapable of handling it. You may find it helpful to include those very phrases in the opening of my prayer. Certainly God doesn't need the reminder, but we often do. No task is too small or too large.
- Supplication: You humbly acknowledge your inability to handle life on your own. You realize you lack the strength and stamina to carry the things you are worrying about. As you wait upon the Lord he will renew your strength.[44] You will find that when you acknowledge through prayer what you can't do, you will grow increasingly dependent on the Lord.
- Thanksgiving: You review God's work in your past. You rehearse the aspects of his character for which you are thankful. You replace worrying with a grateful spirit. Even in the most difficult of circumstances, you can give thanks.[45]

Having walked through the previous three steps, you are prepared to make your prayer requests. Most of us spend the majority of our prayer time on the requests, as if God has to be reminded of our needs. But when Jesus spoke about anxiety, he explicitly stated that our heavenly Father knows what we need.[46] He said,

> Therefore do not be anxious, saying, "What shall we eat?" or "What shall we drink?" or "What shall we wear?" For the Gentiles seek after all these things, and *your heavenly Father knows that you need them all.* But seek first the kingdom of God and his righteousness, and all these things will be added to you [emphasis added].[47]

Jesus encouraged us to change the content of our prayer

requests. Our chief pursuit is no longer relief from anxiety, but rather the kingdom of God and his righteousness. For the anxious person, this is only possible when you prime the pump with the previous three steps: prayer, supplication, and thanksgiving.

After praying with this four-fold pattern found in Philippians 4:6, the Scripture extends to us the promise of 4:7: "And the peace of God, which surpasses all understanding, will guard your hearts and your minds in Christ Jesus."[48] For the person struggling with anxious thoughts, this offers tremendous hope. Who wouldn't want the peace that comes from God himself? It passes our understanding, and it guards our hearts and our minds. However, to be successful at keeping those anxious thoughts at bay, you'll need to read and apply the verse that follows.

Change what you think about.

It's your mind. You are responsible for controlling your thoughts.

To a group of believers whose circumstances were less than perfect,[49] Paul wrote,

> Finally, brothers, whatever is true, whatever is honorable, whatever is just, whatever is pure, whatever is lovely, whatever is commendable, if there is any excellence, if there is anything worthy of praise, think about these things.[50]

The verse lists eight qualities, concluding with the statement, "think on these things." Needless to say, worry and anxiety didn't make the list.

I once had a friend whose father was a brain surgeon. His dad acknowledged that while neurosurgeons had studied the brain for years, and while he had performed countless brain surgeries, there was still so much about it that they didn't understand. One of the things that scientists and philosophers remain unclear about is the connection between the brain and the mind. We need to be careful not to use these words interchangeably, they are actually quite different. When we place the definitions side by side we see those differences more clearly. The brain is an organ of soft nerve tissue contained in the skull that functions as the coordinating centre of sensation and intellectual and nervous activity. On the other hand, the mind is the faculty of consciousness and thought. It designates a person's ability to think, reason, and make determinative choices.[51]

When it comes to anxiety, the distinction between the mind and the brain is essential. Because worrying is so closely associated with your thoughts, we must first answer this question: can we control our thoughts, or are they simply the electronic processes that are a result of certain stimuli upon the soft nervous tissue? While scientists and philosophers will continue the debate,[52] the Bible presents a more definitive answer. You are not a victim, enduring a set of electronic impulses in the expanse between your ears. You can control your thoughts. Consider the following biblical passages:

- For you are not setting your mind on the things of God, but on the things of man.[53]
- We destroy arguments and every lofty opinion raised against the knowledge of God, and take every thought captive to obey Christ.[54]
- For those who live according to the flesh set their minds on the things of the flesh, but those who live according to the Spirit set their minds on the things of the Spirit. For to set the mind on the flesh is death, but

to set the mind on the Spirit is life and peace.[55]

- Have this mind among yourselves, which is yours in Christ Jesus.[56]
- Set your minds on things that are above, not on things that are on earth.[57]

We are commanded to take charge of those thoughts. Furthermore, we will be held responsible for whether or not we do so. I like the word responsible. I can hear two different words in it. I am "response-able." I will be held accountable for my responses because, I am able by the strength which Christ supplies.[58] So, if I'm responsible, how do I bring those thoughts into captivity? The Bible offers two ways: renewing the mind and setting the mind.

Renew Your Mind: Dwelling Upon the Word

The book of Romans may be the most doctrinally intense book in the Bible, but don't let its theological focus fool you; it is also intensely practical. Consider this challenge in Romans 12:2: "Do not be conformed to this world, but be transformed by the renewal of your mind." The word *transformed* comes from the Greek word from which we get metamorphous. It means to change forms. It is used in the transfiguration of Jesus when his robe became bright white.[59] It is used in Romans 12:2 to speak of the changes that are to take place in each of us as believers.[60] This truth gives someone who has fallen repeatedly to the same temptation great hope. You can change. The key is found in the word *renewal*. John MacArthur clarifies,

> The Holy Spirit achieves this transformation by the renewing of the mind, an essential and repeated New Testament theme. The outward transformation is effected by an inner change in the mind, and the Spirit's

means of transforming our minds is the Word. David testified, "Thy word I have treasured in my heart, that I may not sin against Thee."[61] God's own Word is the instrument His own Holy Spirit uses to renew our minds, which, in turn, He uses to transform our living.[62]

Careful study, consistent reading of the Bible, and diligent memorization of biblical passages is the way God promised to renew our minds.[63] I've seen some well-worn Bibles used by those who are battling anxiety. Colored tabs coming off the pages of Scripture for easy reference. I've seen stacks of 3x5 cards, each carrying a verse the worrier was seeking to memorize. This type of renewal is a process. Frankly, we want the change to happen quickly and with minimal effort on our part. Often we dismiss the very pattern that would bring about lasting change because we want the anxiety to stop immediately. We forget that we have spent years succumbing to anxious thoughts. The Scripture will make a difference, but it's going to take more than a verse or two. To aid in this process, you will find passages for comfort on page 64, a 28-day Bible reading schedule on page 65, and 20 biblical passages to memorize on pages 66-67.

Set Your mind: Thinking intentionally

Several times in the Scripture we are encouraged to "set our mind." Paul wrote in Romans,

For those who live according to the flesh set their minds on the things of the flesh, but those who live according to the Spirit set their minds on the things of the Spirit. For to set the mind on the flesh is death, but to set the mind on the Spirit is life and peace.[64]

Some have translated the phrase "set your mind" with one

word: *think*.[65] It's not enough to memorize a verse or read a chapter; you will need to think about these things throughout the day. You must take this idea seriously if you hope to change. It's one thing to say you believe that the Word will renew your mind; it's another thing to give it the opportunity to do so by dwelling on it throughout the day. Bear in mind that your anxious thoughts have become comfortable friends. You may not care much for how they make you feel at the end of the day, but they've been around for awhile. They've made themselves at home in your head. While the Scriptures will renew the mind, you will have to take ownership for what you set your mind upon.

Twenty-five years ago a deeply troubled young man stepped into my office. He was accompanied by a friend for the sake of encouragement. Together they began to pour out his sad story. When he was in 8th grade, he became a victim of sexual abuse at the hand of high school teen. As he entered high school, he struggled with depression, attempted to take his own life, and was hospitalized. He had carried the dark secret alone. Neither parents nor counselors knew his past. Now, seven years later, his anxiety was all-consuming. His struggle with fear and worry had even crept into his sleeping hours, revealing itself through nightmares of the teen who had abused him. I was fresh out of seminary with limited experience in the ministry. As I reached for my Bible, I remember praying to the Lord for guidance. I knew I was in way over my head.

I asked the young man what he was thinking about before he fell asleep. He acknowledged his painful past consumed his thoughts. He said, tearfully, "I'm just praying to God that the nightmares won't come back."

"I understand you're *praying*, but what are you *thinking* about?"

"The nightmares," he said, "I don't know how to stop."

Together we opened up our Bibles to Philippians 4:8 and read,

> Finally, brothers, whatever is true, whatever is honorable, whatever is just, whatever is pure, whatever is lovely, whatever is commendable, if there is any excellence, if there is anything worthy of praise, think about these things.[66]

"Your challenge," I said, "will be to develop a plan where you think on the things that are in that list." Together we read the promise that came next, "What you have learned and received and heard and seen in me—practice these things, and the God of peace will be with you."[67]

"Memorizing is only the first part," I added. "You're actually going to have to do it."

"Do what?" he said.

"Think on these things," I replied.

Together we drew an octagon. He wrote each of the eight qualities found in the verse on the outside boarders of the sign. Inside the sign we wrote the words "Stop! Think on these things." On a separate piece of paper he wrote each quality as the heading for a list. The eight lists would include anything he could think of that was "true, honorable, just, pure, lovely, commendable, excellent, and worthy of praise."

One week later he returned to my office with his friend. The two sat down. I began the conversation. "How's that Bible verse I asked you to memorize?" His friend smiled and shook his head as if he knew something I did not.

"Why the smile?" I asked.

"Did you want him to tell it to you forwards or backwards?"

"Let's start with forwards." I said. The young man quoted the verse perfectly, one word after the other.

"Can you really quote the verse backwards?" I asked incredulously. Phrase by phrase he gave the verse backwards. He didn't miss a beat. "That's pretty amazing" I said. "So how are the nightmares? He looked me in the eyes, shrugged his shoulders, and smiled.

"What nightmares?"

The Third Principle: Desire
Desire God more than relief
from your anxiety

IF A TIME machine existed, there are a few places I would like to travel. I would set the dial for a Monday afternoon in the 1950's. My coordinates would land me in a small room in the back of an English pub on St. Giles Street. The placard at the front door would bear the name "The Eagle and the Child." I would be there for one purpose: to eavesdrop. I would love to listen in on the conversation taking place at the adjoining table where Charles Williams, Hugo Dyson, J.R.R. Tolkien, and C.S. Lewis were conversing over lunch. If such an event were possible, I think I'd become a regular. While it would be seriously cool to hear the earliest renditions of *The Lord of the Rings*, I would be most interested in hearing how C.S. Lewis progressed from being an atheist to becoming one of Christianity's premier apologists. I can't help but believe that at some stage he would begin to articulate one of my favorite quotes about desire:

> It would seem that our Lord finds our desires not too strong, but too weak. We are half-hearted creatures, fooling about with drink and sex and ambition when infinite joy is offered us, like an ignorant child who wants to go on making mudpies in a slum because he cannot imagine what is meant by the offer of a holiday at the sea. We are far too easily pleased.[68]

The anxious person desires nothing so strongly as relief from the anxiety. But what if the pursuit of that relief is nothing more than "making mud pies in the slum?" What if God's plan for you didn't include relief, but a lifelong battle with anxious thoughts so that you might discover the greater joy of dependence on him? What if God, knowing your personal weakness in this area, brought about circumstances that would increase your reliance upon him, rather than take away the problem?[69] It might seem that he was against you, when all the while he would be for you.[70] God wants to offer us more than simple relief from anxiety.[71] He wants to increase our faith.

King David understood this truth. Certainly he had much to worry about, but his counsel in Psalm 37 reveals that he had learned to desire something more than relief from anxiety. Notice his words:

> Don't worry about the wicked or envy those who do wrong. For like grass, they soon fade away. Like spring flowers, they soon wither. Trust in the LORD and do good. Then you will live safely in the land and prosper. Take delight in the LORD, and he will give you your heart's desires. Commit everything you do to the LORD. Trust him, and he will help you.[72]

Two more times in the next several verses David will encourage the reader not to worry.

> Be still in the presence of the LORD, and wait patiently for him to act. Don't worry about evil people who prosper or fret about their wicked schemes. Stop being angry! Turn from your rage! Do not lose your temper—it only leads to harm. For the wicked will be destroyed, but those who trust in the LORD will possess the land.[73]

David warns us three times in the negative: *Don't worry.* Yet, he doesn't stop there. Four times he encourages us in the affirmative: (1) trust in the Lord, (2) take delight in the Lord, (3) commit everything you do to the Lord, and (4) be still in the presence of the Lord. Those four phrases offer you an alternative to desiring only relief from anxiety. They are stepping stones to take you from desiring relief to desiring God.

Trust in the Lord

Perhaps the best known Bible verse about trusting God is found in Proverbs 3:5. "Trust in the Lord with all your heart, and lean not on your own understanding." Eugene Peterson rendered that verse, "Trust GOD from the bottom of your heart; don't try to figure out everything on your own."[74] The anxious person tries to figure it out on his own, and he knows he doesn't have the resources. This is especially evident when we worry about others. Our relationships with our family members is a good example. Parents are prone to worry about their children's future. A sister worries about her brother's drug addiction. A middle-aged woman worries about her aging parents' failing health. When we deal with others' choices, the outcome is outside of our control because their will is their own. We cannot make them want what they don't want for themselves.[75] We can instruct and discipline our children. We can grieve over our siblings' destructive choices. We can lovingly share our concerns with our parents. But in all of these relationships, we cannot ultimately control their will.[76] It is outside the realm of our ability; their future is outside of our field of vision. So we worry. To ultimately gain victory over this type of anxiety, you will need to acknowledge that your resources are limited and trust in the one whose resources are not.

Most of us only trust those with whom we have a meaningful relationship. For instance, if I was looking for someone to hold $1,000 for me while I went away, I would be most confident in the person I knew the best. My ability to trust you (or not) is clearly tied to my knowledge of you, to how well I know your character, intentions, and purposes. It's the same way in our relationship with God. If you are not growing in your knowledge of him who saved you,[77] you will struggle to trust him, and you will succumb again to those feelings of anxiety.

A friend of our family is fond of saying, "If you don't see God as good and loving, you will not be comforted by his sovereignty." Just because the Bible declares that God is in control[78] doesn't mean that I'll trust him. Jesus understood this. He found comfort in trusting his heavenly Father with his future because he had grown in his understanding of his Father's love.[79] If you do not do the same, you will struggle to trust God with the things you value the most. You will attempt to guard them yourself, and in so doing the habit of worrying will return. Trusting God is essential to overcoming worry, and knowing God well is the prerequisite to trusting him completely.

Delight yourself in the Lord

C.S. Lewis embraced atheism at the age of 15. Though raised in a church-going family, he claimed his separation from religion started when he began to see it all as "chore and duty."[80] This is what makes the earlier statement by Lewis so powerful. He discovered that the pursuit of God was worthy of being desired, not simply obligatory. In Psalm 37 King David says the same thing: delight yourself in the Lord. The translators chose the word delight to describe a Hebrew word that means "soft and delicate." It came to mean a life of luxury and enjoyment.[81] Earlier in the Psalms, David ponders delighting in the Lord with eternity in view. He writes, "You make known to me the path of life; in your presence there is fullness of joy; at your right hand are pleasures forevermore."[82] This is what John Piper intends when he changes one word in the Westminster Confession. The 400-year-old document read: "The chief end of man is to glorify God *and* enjoy him forever." But Piper thought it was clearer this way: "The chief end of man is to glorify God *by* enjoying him forever."[83] I agree with Piper. *God is most glorified in us when we are most satisfied with him.*[84]

Finding your delight in the Lord is essential to overcoming anxiety. We have a tendency to be very one-dimensional in our thinking. The more we fixate on relief from anxiety, the more anxious we tend to become. The cares of this world can seem overwhelming; what joy you have will dissipate. But when you begin to find your delight in the Lord, joy will return, and worry will be crowded out. It's hard to be joyful and anxious at the same time. There's a promise connected with the command to delight in the Lord. The text says, "And he will give you the desires of your heart."[85] The word desires could be understood as "requests" or "petitions."[86] When we delight in the Lord, we have turned our desires into prayers.[87] Imagine if each time your heart grew anxious you interpreted it as a signal to bring a prayer request to the Lord. You wouldn't have time to worry. You would be taking your burden to the Lord and leaving it there.[88] When we focus our attention on the Lord like that, we actually end up getting what we desire—the peace of God.

Commit everything you do to the Lord

One summer, when I was child, my family was preparing to go on our summer vacation. Whenever we would take an extended trip, it was my father's habit to pray for safety before we would leave the driveway. As the car came to a stop at the end of our long, gravel lane, my dad asked for a volunteer to pray. My hand was the first one up, so I was granted the responsibility of praying for God's mercies. My parents recall that the bulk of my prayer was spent asking God that we not have an accident on the bridge that was about a half a mile from our home. I'm sure my parents smiled. My dad would later say that while he didn't know what would happen on the trip, he was pretty certain there wouldn't be an accident on the bridge. Oh, the power of a seven year-olds prayer.

When our text says to commit everything to the Lord, it is describing a way, a path, a journey.[89] Kind of like a family vacation, only more like a lifetime than a week. What if I had retained my seven-year-old perspective on prayer throughout my lifetime? What if each morning I paused to commit everything to the Lord for that day's journey? What if I maintained that perspective on prayer throughout the day? What if you did? Perhaps this is what the Bible means when it says, "Pray without ceasing."[90] It's really hard to keep worrying when you're praying without ceasing. This is what prompted William James to say, "The sovereign cure for worry is prayer."[91]

Commit everything to the Lord. He is concerned about the smallest details, and he is capable of handling the largest difficulties.

Be still in the presence of the Lord

When we're anxious, it's hard to be still. We think if we work harder relief from the anxiety will come. But we accomplish one task, only to grow anxious about another. We run faster, only to discover our anxious thoughts were waiting of us at the next destination. We cannot outwork nor outrun our anxious thoughts. This prompted King David to write: "Be still before the Lord and wait patiently on him."[92] Later in the Psalms God speaks in the first person: "Be still and know that I am God. I will be exalted among the nations, I will be exalted in the earth."[93] The Bible ties our ability to be still and wait to what God has done and will do.

Corrie Ten Boom was born in the Netherlands. Her family secretly housed Jews during the Holocaust. Their act of courage would be rewarded with sentences to Nazi prison camps. Corrie and her sister spent years in the prison at Ravensbrück. I've walked the stone pavers at Ravensbrück, laid down by the bleeding hands of women and children. Fresh cut flowers now pour forth from the incinerators, where most prisoners left the facility in the form of smoke and ash. While the barracks are no longer there, the footprints of the foundations serve as a memorial to where thousands would spend their final days. It's hard to imagine living in an environment that must have run rampant with fear and anxiety. Rape and abuse were prevalent; hard labor the only event of the day; death your only escape. Still, this environment would inspire Corrie Ten Boom to write: "Worry is a cycle of inefficient thoughts whirling around a center of fear."

That's an insightful statement worth reading again. *Worry is a cycle of inefficient thoughts whirling around a center of fear.* In the whirling thoughts of worry, it can be difficult to discern what we fear. Our thoughts are too busy. Ultimately, it's not about your busyness, it's about God's faithfulness. It's not about what you do, it's about what he's done. Folk singer Andrew Peterson captures this sentiment in the lyrics of *You Can Rest Easy*:

> *You work so hard to wear yourself down,*
> *And you're running like a rodeo clown.*
> *You're smiling like you're scared to death;*
> *You're out of faith and all out of breath;*
> *You're so afraid you've got nowhere left to go.*
> *Well, you are not alone.*
> *I will always be with you.*
> *You don't have to work so hard;*
> *You can rest easy.*
> *You don't have to prove yourself;*
> *You're already mine.*
> *You don't have to hide your heart;*
> *I already love you.*
> *I hold it in mine.*
> *You can rest easy.*[94]

Stop running. Trust in the Lord. Delight in him. Commit everything you do to him. Be still in his presence. Those four steps are enough to make even the most avid worrier rest easy.

DO WHAT JESUS DID

THE TEACHER looked at the gathering crowd, smiled, and sat down.[95] Gentle breezes were blowing over the hills of Galilee. With the Sea of Galilee as the background, the crowd listened attentively.[96] His instruction held them spellbound. His teaching had started in the local synagogues, but the crowds had grown too large. It wasn't just the locals who gathered now; people were coming from the north[97] and south,[98] traveling those long dusty roads for one purpose: to hear the teacher and be healed by him. The healings were credible; whether the maladies were short-term or long-term, people went away whole again. Sometimes he would touch them, sometimes he would speak, but always they would be healed.

When he taught, though, a different kind of healing took place—a healing of the soul. The destructive behaviors your heart once desired didn't seem so strong anymore. The abuses of your past, not so debilitating. When he spoke, there was hope. Your spirit actually wanted to change.[99] He spoke of a kingdom that was not yet here but that you wanted to be a part of.[100] Always he spoke of change—a change that started first in your thinking, touched your desires, and ultimately effected your behavior. This was so different than the way they had been taught. Their leaders had said that the outside mattered most of all,[101] but this teacher understood that there was something beneath the surface that needed to change first. Not all were pleased with his teaching. Some were hesitant and unwilling to change.

The breeze shifted, as did his teaching. Today, his teaching was even more direct, like he was inside your head helping you see the real cause of your wrong choices. He spoke of how you thought about another man's wife;[102] how you felt about the anger no one knew about.[103] If you had been there that day, you would have been afraid to move, afraid that the slightest shift would be a confession and reveal that he had just addressed your struggle. Suddenly, what you had thought to be your secret, he was now speaking about. Jesus said: *Therefore I tell you, do not be anxious about your life.*

SIX TIMES in the sermon on the mount Jesus spoke about anxiety. His sermon covered a wide variety of topics, and he allotted a sizeable portion to our tendency to worry. While he addresses hypocrisy with a direct rebuke,[104] he addresses our tendency to worry with tender compassion. At the conclusion of this message, the people were astonished at his teaching because he taught them as one having authority.[105] One of the reasons Jesus' teaching had authority was that he lived what taught. The opposite was true of the religious leaders of the day.[106] When Jesus gave advice on overcoming anxiety, we can be confident that he had already taken his own advice and was living it.[107]

If your priorities are divided, focus on the eternal

Jesus opens his teaching on overcoming anxiety with this statement:

> Therefore I tell you, do not be anxious about your life, what you will eat or what you will drink, nor about your body, what you will put on. Is not life more than food, and the body more than clothing?[108]

He understands our tendency to be drawn to things that we can see. He also knows the fleeting nature of the pleasure we find in those things. In the passage that precedes this one, he said,

> Do not lay up for yourselves treasures on earth, where moth and rust destroy and where thieves break in and steal, but lay up for yourselves treasures in heaven, where neither moth nor rust destroys and where thieves do not break in and steal. For where your treasure is, there your heart will be also.[109]

The more we accumulate on this earth, the more we will have a tendency to worry that we might lose it. It seems like we should be able to keep our possessions secure, but Jesus' teaching is clear: we cannot. Thieves break in, moths devour, and rust destroys the remainder.[110] So much of our time is spent worrying about how we can hold on to something that, at best, is only temporary.[111]

Jesus' answer is to focus on what is eternal. This is why he says that you cannot serve God and money.[112] When your heart is divided, you will always have a tendency to worry about the things you can see. The very things you can't take with you.[113] In his book *The Treasure Principle*, Randy Alcorn tells of an experience that made this clear to him.

> The streets of Cairo were hot and dusty. Pat and Rakel Thurman took us down an alley. We drove past Arabic signs to a gate that opened to a plot of overgrown grass. It was a graveyard for American missionaries.
>
> As my family and I followed, Pat pointed to a sun-scorched tombstone that read: "William Borden, 1887-1913." Borden, a Yale graduate and heir to great wealth, rejected a life of ease in order to bring the gospel to Muslims. Refusing to even buy a car, Borden gave

away hundreds of thousands of dollars to missions. After only four months of zealous ministry in Egypt, he contracted spinal meningitis and died at the age of twenty-five.

I dusted off the epitaph of Borden's grave. After describing his love and sacrifices for the kingdom of God and for Muslim people, the inscription ended with a phrase I've never forgotten: *Apart for faith in Christ, there is no explanation for such a life.*

The Thurmans took us straight from Borden's grave to the Egyptian National Museum. The King Tut exhibit was mind-boggling. Tutankhamen, the boy king, was only seventeen when he died. He was buried with solid gold chariots and thousands of golden artifacts. His gold coffin was found within gold tombs within gold tombs within gold tombs. The burial site was filled with tons of gold.

I was struck by the contrast between these two graves. Borden's was obscure, dusty, and hidden off the back alley of a street littered with garbage. Tutankhamen's tomb glittered with unimaginable wealth. Yet where are these two young men now? One, who lived in opulence and called himself king, is in the misery of a Christless eternity. The other, who lived a modest life on earth in service of the one true King, is enjoying his everlasting reward in the presence of his Lord.[114]

If you've forgotten God's faithfulness,
increase your dependence through prayer.

Jesus second warning for the anxious person comes in the form of a question: "Look at the birds of the air: they neither sow nor reap nor gather into barns, and yet your heavenly Father feeds them. Are you not of more value than they?"[115] Later he would make a similar point:

> Therefore do not be anxious, saying, "What shall we eat?" or "What shall we drink?" or "What shall we wear?" For the Gentiles seek after all these things, and your heavenly Father knows that you need them all.[116]

Jesus taught that to worry is to forget the faithfulness of God. He encouraged us to look around at creation. If God was providing for the smallest of creatures, and he knew your needs, shouldn't you anticipate he would meet them?

So how do you maintain your confidence in God's faithfulness? The same way that Jesus did. You grow in dependence upon the Lord through prayer. This is why in the Lord's Prayer we are encouraged to ask God to give us our *daily bread* [emphasis added].[117] We shouldn't let more than 24 hours go by without acknowledging our dependence on him. Jesus himself practiced this and matured in his ability to live this way. In *Just Like Jesus*, I wrote,

> Jesus saw prayer as an expression of dependence on the Father, as a tremendous resource in living life for God's glory. When tempted, he responded, "Man shall not live by bread alone." It's easy to overlook the context of Jesus' statement. He had just completed 40 days of prayer and fasting. His hunger had driven him to a greater level of dependence on the Father. He was so physically weakened that the Father sent angels to restore his strength. Jesus borrowed this statement from Deuteronomy 8:3. There, Moses reminded the Israelites that their parents' hunger should have intensified their dependence on the Lord, but it only became another venue for their complaints. Jesus chose an attitude of dependence over a spirit of complaining. Prayer enabled this choice.[118]

When you worry, you are imagining life on your own. You've forgotten the faithfulness of God. To redevelop your confidence in God's ability to come through, practice praying daily and develop the habit of praying about everything—the big and the small, the important and the mundane, your spiritual needs as well as your physical needs—then review his faithfulness in the past.

If you're doubting his sovereignty, review his promises.

I grew up in Indiana, so I love basketball. But my basketball career came to an abrupt halt when I stopped growing in 8th grade. Jesus said, "Which of you by worrying can add one cubit to his stature?"[119] A cubit is 18 inches. I would have given anything to add a cubit to my height, but no matter how much I dreamed, contrived, or worried, I wasn't adding 18 inches to my stature. The phrase can also be interpreted, "And which of you by being anxious can add a single hour to his span of life?"[120] Whether you wish to add inches to your height or years to your life, worrying won't make a difference. There are just some things that are outside of your control. Fortunately they are not outside of God's control.[121] But when we worry, we doubt that truth.

The theological term we use to describe God's control over all creation is *sovereignty*.[122] Because he preserves,[123] sustains,[124] and governs[125] *all* events, you can be certain that includes the events of your personal life. It is understandable that when difficulties arise you may be tempted to doubt this truth. It often feels like the circumstances in your life are not only painful, but also random. You may feel like the only reasonable option is for you to be anxious about the future. So what are you to do when you struggle to believe that God is in control? Do what Jesus did: review the promises of God that are found in the Scriptures.

The way Jesus endured the crucifixion offers clear testimony that, in spite of his suffering, he was clinging to the promises of God. From our perspective, it's hard to imagine an event that would cause us to doubt the sovereignty of God more than the death of Jesus. On the surface, it appears to be the work of malicious, controlling men. But, as you study Jesus' statements from the cross more carefully, you find that he has drawn each one from the Scriptures.[126] When given an opportunity to doubt his Father's sovereignty over the events of his life, Jesus turned to the promises of Scripture.

Peter points this out in his sermon at Pentecost. He says, "This Jesus, delivered up according to the definite plan and foreknowledge of God, you crucified and killed by the hands of lawless men."[127] Notice the focus on the "definite plan and foreknowledge[128] of God." This speaks of God's sovereign control over the events that took place in Jesus' life. So what did Jesus turn to in the midst of potential confusion and despair? Peter quotes from Psalm 16. Jesus certainly clung to the promise found there:

> For you will not abandon my soul to Hades, or let your Holy One see corruption. You have made known to me the paths of life; you will make me full of gladness with your presence.[129]

Jesus drew his courage to face death with the knowledge that he would shortly be resurrected. He discovered this truth by reviewing the promises of Scripture. This is very practical advice for believers. When we are tempted to doubt the sovereignty of God, we ought to review the promises of God. Our circumstances may be horrific, and the opportunity to doubt God's sovereignty may seem real, but the promises of God can hold at bay the overwhelming anxiety to which we are prone.

Jesus teaches us three vital lessons about anxiety, both through his sermon and through this life: (1) if your priorities are divided, focus on the eternal; (2) if you've forgotten God's faithfulness, increase your dependence on prayer; (3) if you're doubting his sovereignty, review his promises. As you do, you will find that those anxious thoughts about your future will be replaced with hopeful ones.

FOLLOW AS THE SPIRIT LEADS

THE HOLY Spirit is a necessary partner as we develop a biblical strategy for overcoming anxiety. Though an essential resource, he is often an overlooked one.[130] Imagine the anxiety that the disciples would have felt, when, after three years of ministry together, Jesus informed them that he would be leaving.[131] Fortunately, he also promised the disciples that he would send the Holy Spirit so they wouldn't be alone.[132] He said, "I tell you the truth: It is to your advantage that I go away, for if I do not go away, the Helper will not come to you. But if I go, I will send him to you." Jesus chose a great word to describe the third member of the Trinity. He referred to the Spirit as "the Helper." English translators captured his word in other ways: advocate, intercessor, counselor, comforter. The Greek word being translated "helper" is *parakletos*. It is comprised of two ideas: *para*, which means "along side," and *kaleo*, which means "to call forth." Because he is readily available, the Bible describes this relationship as walking in the Spirit. This is instructive; walking is the biblical metaphor to describe daily habits. John MacArthur explains,

> The fact that *peripateo* (walk) is used here in the present tense indicates that Paul is speaking of continuous, regular action, in other words, a habitual way of life. And the fact that the verb is also in the imperative mood indicates he is not giving believers an option but a command. Among other things, walking implies progress, going from where one is to where one ought to be. As a believer submits to the Spirit's control, he moves forward in his spiritual life. Step by step the Spirit moves him from where he is toward where God wants him to be.[133]

The Bible uses the word walk to describe the choices we are making. Because we experience anxiety as a feeling, we often don't think of it as a choice. But walking in the Spirit is not something that happens to us; it is a process we participate in, and it will require a conscientious thought pattern. We will only be able to stop worrying about the future when we learn to think like God thinks today. See pages 68-73 for how steps to bring your thoughts and living under the Spirit's control.

Avoiding *if only* and *what if*

Walking in the Spirit is done in the present tense. Think of it as the *here and now*. Each of us is held captive by time. We cannot change our past, and we do not have complete control over our future. When it comes to anxiety, we experience its effects in the here and now, but it is actually the result of thinking unproductively about our past or our future. For most who struggle with anxiety, this process has become so habitual that they may not even realize they are doing it. Two sets of words serve as reminders that we are entering into that unproductive thinking.[134] The words that signify our return to the past are *if only*, and the words that indicate we are worrying about the future are *what if*. Obsessing about our past failures or worrying about future events has a paralyzing effect on our minds. It keeps us from giving our best effort to walk with the Spirit in the here and now.

Don't forget the redemptive nature of the Gospel

If only is the phrase that is used when you worry about the effects of your past. You find yourself so chained to the events of your yesterdays, that you cannot give your best effort to opportunities that occur today. Perhaps you've had these thoughts:

- *If only* my first marriage hadn't failed, I wouldn't have these struggles with my kids.
- *If only* I had studied more in college, I wouldn't have been overlooked for the promotion.
- *If only* my spouse hadn't been unfaithful, I would trust others more.
- *If only* I would have controlled my temper in the past, I would be closer to my family.
- *If only* I hadn't wasted those years in my life, I would be more successful now.

Such thinking, if practiced, will become habitual. But it is patently untrue because you are not taking into account the redemptive nature of the gospel.[135] While there certainly may be ongoing consequences for the decisions of your past, the Bible's story is one of redemption. It tells of lives lived badly that became instruments for good. It speaks of sins committed that were forgiven. It is not a book of one-and-done opportunities; it is one of second chances.[136] The word *redeemed* means to buy back.[137] To be redeemed means that Christ's death on the cross paid the penalty for my sin. I no longer owe the debt to God for my wrongful pattern of living. Peter captured it best:

> Knowing that you were not redeemed with corruptible things, like silver or gold, from your aimless conduct received by tradition from your fathers, but with the precious blood of Christ, as of a lamb without blemish and without spot. [138]

The gospel frees us from the attitudes and actions that seemed so enslaving in our past. Consider this passage in

1 Corinthians 6:9-11:

> Or do you not know that the unrighteous will not inherit the kingdom of God? Do not be deceived: neither the sexually immoral, nor idolaters, nor adulterers, nor men who practice homosexuality, nor thieves, nor the greedy, nor drunkards, nor revilers, nor swindlers will inherit the kingdom of God. *And such were some of you. But you were washed, you were sanctified, you were justified in the name of the Lord Jesus Christ and by the Spirit of our God* [emphasis added].

Whatever your attitude, thought, or behavior from your past, redemption makes possible genuine change. When you come to faith in Christ, you are cleansed, set apart and placed into a right relationship with God. The words, *and such were some of you*, remind us that we are not chained to the sinful choices of our past or the sinful actions that may have been done to us. When we say "*If only* this hadn't happened, I wouldn't be anxious," we are not taking into account the redemptive nature of the Gospel.

Walking in the Spirit means that when I look at my past, I don't see my failure alone. My past failures are set in the new context of having been redeemed. This new context allows me to learn from my failures without being debilitated by them.

Don't assume you know the future

When you worry about the future, you set your mind on uncertain things. You cannot know whether these events will come to pass or not; you can only assume they will. To worry is to center your imagination around possibilities, not realities. Once activated, your imagination swings into overdrive. It's easy to think of additional things that could go wrong. The more you worry, the greater the possibilities. To break the cycle, you will need to acknowledge a crucial assumption: Only God possesses the wisdom to know all things actual and possible. When we use the words *what if*, we are assuming we can be like him. It may not feel like pride, but it is. Perhaps you've used these phrases:

- *What if* I lose my job because of this poor economy?
- *What if* I never get married? Can I still be happy?
- *What if* my children are not successful when they grow up?
- *What if* I can't have children?
- *What if* my retirement runs out before my life does?

Only God can know all realities and possibilities. To assume that we have that degree of knowledge reveals our arrogance. God's wisdom is best defined in this way: God knows all things actual and possible and what is best for me.[139] When the children of Israel departed Egypt, the Bible records, "God did not lead them by way of the land of the Philistines, although that was near. For God said, 'Lest the people change their minds when they see war and return to Egypt.'"[140] God made a decision to lead the people by way of the Red Sea because he knew the possibility of their fear as if it were a reality.[141] Such is the wisdom of God. At best we can guess about the future, but God knows all things actual and possible.

The crossing of the Red Sea became a defining moment for the nation of Israel, but imagine the anxiety in the moments before God split the Red Sea and made a way of escape. You can almost hear them say, "*What if* the Egyptians attack us? *What if* we can't protect our wives and children? *What if* we never make it to the Promised Land? *What if* we die in the wilderness? We should have stayed in the land of Egypt."

The words *what if* look to a future we cannot see. Those words assume that we know what only God can know. Because we cannot know the future, our thoughts about the future are often anxious ones. We worry about what we don't know, as opposed to trusting in the One who does.

Not every use of *what if* means that we're worrying. These are also the words that we use when we plan for the future. However, if we have an obsession with potential future events; if we use the words frequently—particularly about events that we cannot control—then we are choosing anxiety over trusting God. Now when I hear the words *what if* in my head, they sound a warning signal, reminding me that I'm worrying about my future instead of trusting God with it.

Practicing a new way of thinking

Earlier I wrote of a paradigm that has been effective for me and helpful to others attempting to change habitual thought patterns. I have often recommended that anxious people start by developing a new think list, replacing anxious thoughts with biblical ones. Philippians 4:8 is a great place to start. There we read:

> Finally, brothers, whatever is true, whatever is honorable, whatever is just, whatever is pure, whatever is lovely, whatever is commendable, if there is any excellence, if there is anything worthy of praise, *think about these things* [emphasis added].

That final phrase is a command, not simply a consideration. The reason we often view it as optional is that the task of changing our thinking seems too overwhelming. After all, we reason, how can we overturn years of anxious thinking by simply meditating on a few words? We change our habitual thinking the same way that we developed it: one thought at a time.

The believer has the distinct advantage of the Holy Spirit enabling this process. As we take the first step by faith, he enables us to take future steps. The Holy Spirit makes change possible, but he does this in cooperation with us. In *Dead-End Desires* I wrote about this process as a crossroads.

> Imagine yourself at a crossroads. There are only two paths from which to choose. [...] Applying the Word for change is what happens every time you make that choice at the crossroads. Often your feelings will be drawing you one way, but by faith you will need to choose the other. Eventually the new habit will become instinctive, and you will keep in step with the Spirit more naturally. In the beginning, developing this habit will take a concentrated effort.[142]

Don't be overwhelmed by the whole process, simply take it a step at a time. Open your Bible to Philippians 4:8 and take a look at your new think list. Then, draw an octagon and write one quality from the verse on each side of the octagon (there are eight qualities in Philippians 4:8). Inside the octagon, write "Stop! Think on these things." Use the Philippians 4:8 stop sign as a reminder of where you should be setting your thoughts. When your thoughts wander beyond those parameters, choose to bring them back.

Dwell upon the new thoughts. Like a stroke victim learning to walk again, you will need to tell your mind what to do.

BRAVING THE STORM

AT THE Battle of Waterloo, Lord Wellington Booth's British army defeated Napoleon's French forces. When Booth was asked if he believed the British were braver than the French he is reported to have said, "We were not braver than the French. We were just braver five minutes longer."

Anxiety, worry, and fear are formidable foes. They will not go away without a fight, and your fight may be lifelong. Others before you have fought in this conflict and continued the battle in spite of their challenges. Martin Luther struggled with debilitating fear; Charles Haddon Spurgeon battled depression, but both were used by God.

This book was not intended to keep you out of the storms of anxiety, but to help you find safe shelter when you pass through them. When you're anxious, return to your biblical strategies. Think like God thinks. Do what Jesus did. Submit to the Spirit's leading.

In John Bunyan's *Pilgrim's Progress*, Hopeful passes over the final river without difficulty, while Christian fights the whole way to keep his head above water. Nevertheless, both reached their final destination. God is taking you on a journey. Your path may be darker than others', but it is doable. Not because of your strength, but because of his power. Not because of your plans, but because of his wisdom. Not because of who you are, but just because he loves you too much to leave you where you are. As you trust him, you can remain safe in the storm.

> *And I am sure of this, that he who began a good work in you will bring it to completion at the day of Jesus Christ.*
> Philippians 1:6

How to Apply What You've Learned

The discovery of new truths is the beginning of change, but discovery by itself cannot accomplish real change. To do that, you will need to replace your old habits with new ones, your old ideas with more accurate ones, and your old thoughts with more biblical ones. The final pages of this booklet are dedicated to helping you establish those new habits. Prayer, Scripture, and the Holy Spirit were the divine resources that Jesus used, and those same resources are available to you and me today.

(1) Prayer

Whatever the struggle, we have a tendency to see prayer as a panic button—we hit it only when we're in need. Yet, the Bible has over 650 examples of prayer. These are an excellent resource for growth in your prayer life. The following pages offer two different prayer patterns and a listing of the names of God.

(2) Scripture

A growing understanding of and confidence in God is essential to overcoming anxiety. Three attributes of God are particularly worth noting: his love, power, and wisdom. I have provided 28 days of Bible readings in these areas. To aid with Scripture retrieval, I have included 20 biblical passages to memorize that apply directly to anxiety and worry.

(3) The Spirit

Dependence on the Spirit is essential for overcoming anxiety. Developing new habits by walking in the Spirit is the means through which we express that daily dependence.

The 10 Minute Prayer Pattern: PRAY

The *PRAY* acrostic is a memory device for prayer. It can be as short as a few minutes, or may include more time as God leads. PRAY stands for Praise, Repent, Ask, and Yield.

(1) Praise

At the beginning of prayer, praise the *who*, *what*, and *why* of God. Remember *who* he is by reflecting upon his character. When you remember *what* he's done, you are meditating on his works. Finally, remember the *why* of God. He is motivated by his steadfast love towards us (Psa. 100:5).

(2) Repent

Once you've thought about what God has done, you can move easily to what *you* haven't done. Repentance takes place when we remember our failures and turn from them. A humble confession in prayer reveals a dependence on the Spirit in order to be restored to God. True repentance includes my actions and attitudes (Phil. 2:5).

(3) Ask

Jesus taught us to *ask* of God, and Paul gave us a great prayer list to follow (see Col. 1:9-12). The spiritual nature of the prayers of Scriptures are helpful in praying for yourself and others.

(4) Yield

Jesus grew to the point where he could say, "Not my will but yours be done." Yielding your desires (as hard as that may initially be) is an essential element of prayer. Once you've made known your requests, make sure you surrender your desires.

Psalm 139:23-24 - A Song of Trust

Psalm 139 can be understood as a *song of trust*. The final verses of Psalm 139 form an excellent paradigm of prayer for the anxious person. "Search me, O God, and know my heart; try me and know my anxious thoughts; and see if there be any hurtful way in me, and lead me in the everlasting way"(Ps. 139:23-24, NASV). Build your prayer time around these phrases: (1) search me, (2) know me, (3) try me, (4) lead me.

(1) Search me

Rather than asking the Lord to remove your anxiety, ask him to search you. The word means a diligent, difficult probing.[143] There is an obvious attempt at transparency in this request. You will never gain victory over our anxious thoughts as long as you hide them. Read Psalm 139:1-16 to see the thoroughness of God's knowledge when he searches your heart. Start your prayer with *search me*, and then quietly wait for him to reveal what needs to change.

(2) Know me

One of the challenges with anxiety is that we feel alone in the struggle. We worry because we think no one else is paying attention to our situation. We tell ourselves that if others only knew, they'd understand. When we say to the Lord, "Know me," we are admitting that someone knows us better than we know ourselves. At the same time, we are acknowledging our desire for this full and complete knowledge to be used in whatever way is best. The Hebrew word of *know* is *yada*. We immediately recognize this word in our culture from the phrase *yada, yada, yada*. You can almost hear someone impatiently droning, *I know, I know, I know*. When, through prayer, God begins to reveal areas you ought to change, avoid an I-know-it-all attitude. Growing in prayer means developing a teachable spirit.

(3) Try me

David cried out, "Try me and know my anxious thoughts." (Ps. 139:23). While it is difficult to imagine, coming to this point in your prayer life is essential when you struggle with anxiety. David isn't the only biblical writer who asked the Lord to test him. (Ps. 7:9; Pro. 17:3; Jer. 11:20; 1 Thes. 2:4). If you know anxiety firsthand, consider the irony. We are often trying to avoid situations where we are susceptible to stress and worry, and we pray to that end. But David had progressed in prayer to the point where he prayed that God would test him with such challenges. The purpose of the "try me" request is found in the phrase that follows it. "And see if there be any hurtful way in me" (Ps. 139:23). Have you considered how your anxiety may be hurting others? A spouse? Your children? The family next door? This is why we ask the Lord to test us and reveal our anxious thoughts.

(4) Lead me

Having worked through the earlier steps of prayer, David asked the Lord "to lead him in the everlasting way"(Ps. 139:24). We learned from Jesus' example that when we struggle with anxiety, we ought to sharpen our focus on eternity. Pray that way. Don't just look for relief from your present anxieties. Use your prayer life to look further down the road. Catch a glimpse of eternity and humbly allow the Lord to lead you in the way that best prepares you for your eternal home. (John 14:1-6; Ps. 16:11).

Rehearsing the Names of God

When we're anxious, our thoughts are too much on ourselves. Even our prayer life can become self-centered. One of the ways to avoid this error is to deliberately incorporate God's names in your prayer time. To get started, choose one name a day and reflect upon it as you pray.

GOD, MIGHTY CREATOR - *ELOHIM*
THE GOD WHO SEES ME - *EL ROI*
GOD ALMIGHTY - *EL SHADDAY*
THE EVERLASTING GOD/THE ETERNAL GOD - *EL OLAM*
THE LORD WILL PROVIDE - *YAHWEH YIREH*
LORD - *YAHWEH*
LORD, MASTER - *ADONAY*
THE LORD WHO HEALS - *YAHWEH ROPHE*
THE LORD MY BANNER - *YAHWEH NISSI*
CONSUMING FIRE, JEALOUS GOD - *ESH OKLAH, EL KANNA*
HOLY ONE OF ISRAEL - *QEDOSH YISRAEL*
THE LORD IS PEACE - *YAHWEH SHALOM*
THE LORD OF HOSTS - *YAHWEH TSEBAOTH*
THE LORD MY ROCK - *YAHWEH TSURI*
THE LORD IS MY SHEPHERD - *YAHWEH ROI*
THE NAME - *HASHEM*
KING - *MELEK*
HUSBAND - *ISH*
LIVING GOD - *EL CHAY*
DWELLING PLACE - *MAON*
REFUGE - *MACHSEH*
SHIELD - *MAGEN*
FORTRESS - *METSUDA*
STRONG TOWER - *MGIDAL OZ*
JUDGE - *SHOPHET*
HOPE OF ISRAEL - *MIQWEH YISRAEL*
THE LORD OUR RIGHTEOUSNESS - *YAHWEH TSID QENU*
GOD MOST HIGH - *EL ELYON*
THE LORD IS THERE - *YAHWEH SHAMMAH*
FATHER - *AB, ABBA, PATER*

Taken from *Praying the Names of God - A Daily Guide* [144]

Passages of Comfort & Psalms for the Anxious

Suggestions for reading: key passages and Psalms

Passages of Comfort

The following passages were selected with anxiety in mind. Consider writing them on 3x5 cards for easy access.

Deuteronomy 31:6, NLT
Job 23:10
Proverbs 16:6
Isaiah 30:18
Isaiah 40:28-31
Isaiah 41:10-13
Isaiah 43:1-3
Isaiah 46:9, 10, NLT
Jeremiah 29:11
Lamentations 3:22, 23, 31-33
Zephaniah 3:17
Matthew 6:25-34
Matthew 11:28-30
John 6:37
Romans 8:1, 28, 31-39
2 Corinthians 1:10
2 Corinthians 4:16-18
2 Corinthians 5:1-10
Ephesians 3:20, 21
Philippians 1:6, 21-22
Philippians 4:6-9
1 Thessalonians 5:23
2 Thessalonians 2:16, 17
2 Timothy 1:7
Hebrews 2:18
Hebrews 4:14-16
Hebrews 13;5, 6
1 Peter 5:6, 7
1 John 4:18
Revelation 21:3-6

Psalms for the Anxious

The Psalms are an excellent resource to curb anxiety's attack. Tab the page in your Bible, then highlight the verse for quick reference.

Psalm 3:3-6
Psalm 5:11, 12
Psalm 9:10
Psalm 14:5, 6
Psalm 16:5-8, NLT
Psalm 17:6-9
Psalm 18:1-6, 30-32
Psalm 25:2, 3
Psalm 27:1, 2, 13, 14
Psalm 28:6, 7
Psalm 30:2, 3
Psalm 31:1, 7, 8
Psalm 31:19
Psalm 33:4
Psalm 34:10, 18
Psalm 37:23,24
Psalm 57:1-3
Psalm 65:5
Psalm 68:19, 20
Psalm 69:32, 33
Psalm 86:5
Psalm 91
Psalm 94:18-19
Psalm 103:1-14
Psalm 109:21, 22, 26, 27
Psalm 118:5-9, 14
Psalm 121
Psalm 139:1-18
Psalm 145: 14

28 Daily Bible Readings for Anxiety

These readings focus on the love of God, the power of God, and the wisdom of God. See the diagram and explanation on page 70.

DAILY READINGS   DAILY APPLICATION

THE LOVE OF GOD

Day 1: Psalm 25:1-22
Day 2: Psalm 34:1-24
Day 3: Psalm 86:1-17
Day 4: Psalm 103:1-22
Day 5: Psalm 106:1-48
Day 6: Isaiah 54:4-14
Day 7: Romans 5:6-11
Day 8: Romans 8:31-37
Day 9: Deut. 7:6-11
Day 10: Luke 15:11-24
Day 11: Ephesians 3:15-19
Day 12: 1 John 4:7-11
Day 13: John 15:9-17

As you read these Bible passages consider: (1) How is God's love expressed in this passage? (2) In what ways has God shown his love to me personally? (3) How should my attitude/actions change today as I dwell upon God's love for me?

THE POWER OF GOD

Day 14: Psalm 8-9
Day 15: Psalm 97:1-12
Day 16: Psalm 148:1-14
Day 17: Job 41-42
Day 18: Jeremiah 32:16-27
Day 19: Ephesians 3:14-21
Day 20: Revelation 4-5

As you read these Bible passages consider: (1) How is God's power revealed in this passage? (2) What should be my response when I consider God's power?

THE WISDOM OF GOD

Day 21: Psalm 19:1-14
Day 22: Psalm 104:1-35
Day 23: Psalm 139:1-24
Day 24: Proverbs 1:1-7
Day 25: Isaiah 46:9-13
Day 26: Matthew 6:25-34
Day 27: Romans 11:33-36
Day 28: 1 Cor. 2:6-16

As you read these Bible passages consider: (1) How is God's wisdom revealed in this passage? (2) What should be my response to God's wisdom? (3) What steps can I take to better apply God's wisdom?

The Scripture Retrieval Method

The Scripture retrieval method is based upon three premises: (1) Scripture provides an excellent *defense* against temptation. This is why the first ten verses listed below are learned in the lie/truth formula to defend against temptation. (2) Scripture provides an excellent *offense* to weaken temptation's appeal. This is why the second ten verses are learned about the character of God and the nature of the Gospel. Loving God well and appreciating the Gospel weakens the draw of temptation. (3) We learn the Scriptures best when we *understand* the words we are memorizing and *apply* them to our real life challenges. For this reason, memory alone is an ineffective means of defending against sin.

Biblical Truths to Combat the Deceiver's Lies

Lie 1: God isn't enough. You need something more. Truth: Psalm 73:25-26

Lie 2: If God *did* love you, your life wouldn't be so hard. Truth: Romans 5:3-4

Lie 3: God doesn't really care about you. That's why you have to worry. Truth: 1 Peter 5:7

Lie 4: If your circumstances were different, you wouldn't worry like you do. Truth: Philippians 4:11-12

Lie 5: You can't control these anxious thoughts. There's nothing you can do about them.
Truth: Psalm 42:11; Colossians 3:2

Lie 6: What if God is keeping something good from you? Truth: Psalm 84:10-12

Lie 7: Your parents struggled with anxiety, so you will too. Truth: Ezekiel 18:20

Lie 8: Don't let anyone know you're anxious. You can handle this by yourself.
　　Truth: Proverbs 28:13; James 5:16
Lie 9: If you feel alone, you must *be* alone.
　　Truth: Deuteronomy 31:6, NLT
Lie 10: What if what happened before happens again?
　　Truth: Matthew 6:34; 2 Corinthians 12:9

Biblical Promises about God and the Gospel

Promise 1: God is working all things for my good.
　　Passage: Romans 8:28
Promise 2: God loves me and enjoys acting on my behalf.
　　Passage: Zephaniah 3:17
Promise 3: God will be my help in my time of need.
　　Truth: Psalm 121:1, 2
Promise 4: Nothing can separate me from the love of God.
　　Passage: Romans 8:35, 37
Promise 5: God is purposefully at work in my life and circumstances. Passage: Jeremiah 29:11, 13
Promise 6: God will be with me in my trials. I am not alone.
　　Passage: Isaiah 43:2
Promise 7: God will strengthen me when I am weak.
　　Passage: Isaiah 41:10, 13
Promise 8: God's wisdom surpasses mine.
　　Passage: Isaiah 55:9
Promise 9: Nothing is too difficult for God.
　　Passage: Jeremiah 32:27
Promise 10: God will provide comfort when I am anxious.
　　Passage: Psalm 94:18-19

Visit biblicalstrategies.com to order these 20 memory verse cards with helpful commentary on the back of each card.

Suggestions for Spirit controlled thoughts: the stop sign

The Philippians 4:8 Stop Sign

Philippians 4:8 serves as an excellent reminder for how we ought to think. Think of the eight qualities listed in the passage as forming the sides of a stop sign. Then, practice keeping your thoughts within those parameters. As your thoughts wander outside of these limits (i.e. worrying about a future event or confrontation), draw your mind back in and review the eight qualities. It may be beneficial to create columns, then, using the biblical words as the heading, list the things that are true, honorable, just, etc.

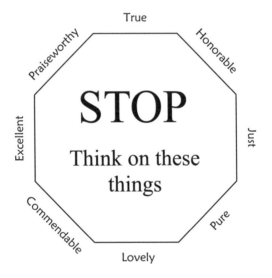

Finally, brothers, whatever is true, whatever is honorable, whatever is just, whatever is pure, whatever is lovely, whatever is commendable, if there is any excellence, if there is anything worthy of praise, think about these things.
Philippians 4:8

8 Thought Filters and Questions

Thought Filters:	Ask Yourself:
True	Is what I'm thinking *true* about God, particularly his fatherly care for me?
Honorable	Do my thoughts honor God? Do they reflect the knowledge that he is wonderful, kind, loving, wise, and powerful?
Right/Just	Are my thoughts holy, righteous, or just? Are they the kind that the Lord himself would think?
Pure	Do my thoughts cast doubt on God's goodness or the truth of his promises? Do they elevate my own importance or desire?
Lovely	Do my thoughts flow from a heart filled with tenderness and affection for the Lord? Would my thoughts bring him pleasure?
Commendable	Are my thoughts of good repute? Are they grounded in faith?
Excellent	Do my thoughts cause me to be fearful, or do they fill my heart with courage and strong commitment to virtuous living?
Praiseworthy	Would the Lord commend my thoughts? Would they bring him glory?

Taken from *Overcoming Fear, Worry, and Anxiety*[145]

God's Character and You

Anxiety is the natural result of doubting the character of God. This diagram helps you think properly about God's character in relation to your well-being. God's wisdom means he *knows* what is best for you; God's power means he has the *ability* to accomplish what is best for you; God's love means that he genuinely *wants* what is best for you. Reflecting upon this triad is a helpful way to overcome anxiety. Whatever storm you face, you are safe within the confines of God's love, wisdom, and power.

Anxiety will occur whenever you doubt one of these elements of God's character. The diagram is also an excellent diagnostic tool for anxiety. It clarifies where you should focus your Bible study. For instance, if you doubt God's goodness, then study passages about his love. If you question his ability, choose passages on his power. If you question whether he knows what is best, then study passages on his wisdom.

The Three Circles of Clarification[146]

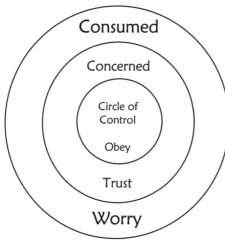

The Circle of Control

The inner circle is the circle of control because it includes the elements over which you are able to exercise control and have been given responsibility. You'll note that it is the smallest circle; there is very little in this life that you and I can actually control. For instance, I can't control the traffic on my way to work, but I can control my *response* to that traffic. I can't control the world's economy, but I can control my spending and be fiscally responsible. I can't control the outcome of my children's choices, but I am able to control the instruction and discipline I give to them while they are under my authority. God has intentionally made my circle of responsibility the smallest. His Word gives precepts and commands so that I can know what my responsibilities are and obey him accordingly. As I walk in the Spirit, and not in the flesh, I am able to do everything that is within this circle (Gal. 5:16, Phil. 4:13).

Concerned

The middle circle contains the areas that touch my life, but over which I exercise limited control. A friend or a family member who is living a dangerous life style would fall into this category. Hopefully, through the years, my compassion and loyalty have won me the opportunity to speak to him about my concerns. Certainly, I have influence as a friend. Still, I have to remember, I do not ultimately control his choices or the outcome of those choices. He alone is responsible. He, too, has a circle of control.

In the areas where I feel concern, I pray and look for opportunities to minister. But when I think I can control my friend's choices, I become manipulative. I use tools like shame or silence. I bribe him by holding our relationship hostage. To avoid this pattern, I remind myself of my responsibilities as found in 2 Timothy.

> And the Lord's servant *must not be quarrelsome but kind to everyone, able to teach, patiently enduring evil, correcting his opponents with gentleness.* God may perhaps grant them repentance leading to a knowledge of the truth, and they may come to their senses and escape from the snare of the devil, after being captured by him to do his will [emphasis added](2 Tm. 2:24-26).

Ultimately, I cannot make my friend change his mind. Only the Spirit of God can bring about repentance. In the areas where I am concerned, but cannot control, I must learn to trust God. This is why prayer is a valuable replacement for worry. Every time I pray, I am trusting God to do in another's life what I cannot do.

Consumed

Even when I am not manipulative, it is easy to drift

from the middle circle into the outer one. Being *concerned* is only one step a way from being *consumed*. I go to sleep thinking about a situation and wake up with it on my mind. It distracts me from the important conversations around me. It interrupts my relationship with God, and it intrudes upon my relationships with others. This is the circle of worry. I can't seem to get my mind off the matter at hand. When I am in this circle, it feels like I should be able to come up with a solution if I only worry for a little longer. That is anxiety's lie. Without realizing it, I have drifted from being concerned to being consumed.

The three circles clarify an inherent danger when we move from the inner circle to the outer. The outer circle does not touch the inner. That means, when I am worrying about a matter, I cannot fulfill my God-given responsibilities. My time and energies are wasted in the *consumed* circle, and I have nothing left to spend on the areas that I am responsible for. This is why unchecked anxiety often leads to other sins. We've depleted the resources that God had given us to fulfill our responsibilities today because we were worrying about tomorrow. Jesus made this case in his Sermon on the Mount when he said, "Therefore do not be anxious about tomorrow, for tomorrow will be anxious for itself. Sufficient for the day is its own trouble" (Mat. 6:34).

When something or someone is beginning to consume your mind, the three circles serve as a vivid reminder that you are not fulfilling your responsibilities. Stop obsessing over what you can't control and give your best efforts to those areas that you can. Be faithful to do what God has asked of you.

NOTES

1. Galatians 2:12
2. Peter seems bold when he gets out of the boat and attempts to walk on the water, but a few steps and the fear returns (Matt. 14:22-33).
3. Luke 5:10
4. Luke 5:8
5. Luke 5:10
6. Matthew 14:27
7. Matthew 14:30
8. Luke 22:61
9. Psalm 142;4, 5
10. Mark 4:37, 38
11. *Just Like Jesus*, 28.
12. 1 Peter 5:6,7
13. Daniel 4:35; Romans 11:33-36
14. 1 Peter 5:8
15. 1 Thessalonians 5:6, 8; 2 Timothy 4:5; 1 Peter 1:13; 4:7, 5:8
16. W.E. Vine, *Vine's Expository Dictionary of New Testament Words* (Mclean, VA: Macdonald Publishing, 1989).
17. Matthew 6:33
18. Romans 12:2
19. Philippians 4:6
20. indicative mood
21. subjunctive mood
22. imperative mood
23. Jerry Bridges, *Respectable Sins* (Colorado Springs, CO: Navpress, 2007), 64-65.
24. *Just Like Jesus: biblical strategies for growing well*, 46-47.
25. 1 John 1:9
26. Philippians 4:6
27. Philippians 4:6-7
28. Matthew 10:29
29. Psalm 139:16-18
30. http://oceancity.patch.com/articles/beach-replenishment-how-does-it-work#photo-13910472
31. Mark 14:36
32. Psalm 102:25-28
33. Daniel 4:35
34. G. Kittel, G. Friedrich, & G.W. Bromiley, *Theological Dictionary of the New Testament* (Grand Rapids, MI: W.B. Eerdmans, 1985).
35. 1 Peter 5:7
36. http://www.nimh.nih.gov/statistics/1ANYANX_ADULT.shtml
37. Luke 22:31-32
38. To develop your personal praise journal see *Dead-End Desires: biblical strategies for overcoming self-pity*, 61-62.
39. Job 1:21
40. Lamentations 3:21-24
41. Philippians 4:10-13
42. Philippians 4:13, NLT
43. 2 Corinthians 12:7
44. Isaiah 40:31
45. Philippians 4:4
46. Matthew 6:32
47. Matthew 6:31-33
48. Philippians 4:7
49. Paul promised the Philippians that God would supply all their needs. This is a vivid reminder that they had given from the depth of their poverty, not their wealth.
50. Philippians 4:8
51. C. Soanes & A. Stevenson, *Concise Oxford English Dictionary* (Oxford: Oxford University Press, 2004).
52. http://www.scribd.com/doc/2451851/Is-There-a-Difference-Between-the-Mind-and-Brain
53. Matthew 16:23

54. 2 Corinthians 10:5
55. Romans 8:5-6
56. Philippians 2:5
57. Colossians 3:2
58. Philippians 4:13, NASV
59. Matthew 17:2; Mark 9:2

60. The verb *transformed* "is a present passive imperative. Although God brings about the transformation, we must voluntarily place ourselves at his disposal so it can happen. He will not 'transform' us against our will. The present tense suggests that the process is to continue throughout life. Transformation is not instantaneous" (R.H. Mounce, The New American Commentary: Romans (Nashville, TN: Broadman & Holman Publishers, 1995)).

61. Psalm 119:11
62. John MacArthur, *MacArthur New Testament Commentary: Romans* (Chicago, IL: Moody Press, 1991).
63. Psalm 19
64. Romans 8:5-6
65. John MacArthur, *The MacArthur Study Bible* (Wheaton, IL: Crossway Books, 1997).
66. Philippians 4:8
67. Philippians 4:9
68. *The Weight of Glory, and Other Addresses.*
69. 2 Corinthians 12:9-10
70. James 1:2-4
71. Matthew 6:33
72. Psalm 37:1-5, NLT
73. Psalm 37:7-9, NLT
74. Eugene Peterson, *The Message: The Bible in Contemporary Language* (Colorado Springs, CO: NavPress, 2005).
75. A conversation with Dr. Nicholas Ellen.
76. 2 Timothy 2:24-26
77. 2 Peter 3:18
78. Daniel 4:34-35

79. John 15:9. See also *Dead-End Desires: biblical strategies for overcoming self-pity*, 37-40.

80. http://en.wikipedia.org/wiki/C._S._Lewis

81. F. Brown, S.R. Driver, & C.A. Briggs, *The Enhanced Brown-Driver-Briggs Hebrew and English Lexicon* (Oak Harbor, WA: Logos Research Systems, 2000), 772.

82. Psalm 16:11
83. http://www.desiringgod.org/dg/id87.htm
84. http://www.desiringgod.org/resource-library/sermons/god-is-most-glorified-in-us-when-we-are-most-satisfied-in-him
85. Psalm 16:11

86. J. Strong, *The New Strong's Dictionary of Hebrew and Greek Words* (Nashville, TN: Thomas Nelson, 1996).

87. D. A. Carson, *New Bible commentary: 21st Century Edition* (Downers Grove, IL: Inter-Varsity Press, 1994).

88. 1 Peter 5:7

89. R. L. Harris, G. L. Archer, Jr. & B. K. Waltke, *Theological Wordbook of the Old Testament* (Chicago, IL: Moody Press, 1999), 196-197.

90. 1 Thessalonians 5:17
91. http://quotationsbook.com/quotes/tag/worry/#sthash.f4GdqosW.dpbs
92. Psalm 37:7
93. Psalm 46:10
94. Lyrics by Andrew Peterson © 2012.
95. Matthew 5:1
96. This is my imaginative retell-

ing of the Sermon on the Mount. The historical record is found in Matthew 5-7.

97. Matthew 4:24
98. Matthew 4:25
99. John 6:68
100. See *The English Standard Study Bible*.
101. Matthew 6:2, 5, 16
102. Matthew 5:27-30
103. Matthew 5:21-26
104. Matthew 6:2, 5, 16
105. Matthew 7:29
106. Matthew 7:28-29
107. James 1:22
108. Matthew 6:25
109. Matthew 6:19-21
110. Matthew 6:19

111. In the parable of the sower, Jesus makes this clear. The third soil in his illustration springs up with thorns, and it crushes out the appeal of the gospel message in that person's life. Pay careful attention to what Jesus compares to the thorns. "As for what was sown among thorns, this is the one who hears the word, but the cares of the world and the deceitfulness of riches choke the word, and it proves unfruitful" (Matt. 13:22). This further confirms the more temporal things we possess the greater our tendency towards worry.

112. Matthew 6:24
113. Hebrews 11:1-3
114. Randy Alcorn, The Treasure Principle (Colorado Springs, CO: Multnomah Books, 2001), 36-38.
115. Matthew 6:26
116. Matthew 6:31-32
117. Matthew 6:11
118. *Just Like Jesus*, 19.
119. Matthew 6:27, NKJV
120. Matthew 6:27, ESV
121. Daniel 4:35
122. Psalm 139
123. Hebrews 1:3
124. Ephesians 1:11
125. Psalm 103:19; Daniel 4:35
126. Compare: Luke 23:34 with Leviticus 5:14-16; Luke 23:43 with Psalm 73:23-26; John 19:26-27 with Exodus 20:12; Matthew 27:46 with Psalm 22:1-4; John 19:28 with Psalm 69:21; John 19:30 with Isaiah 53:10, 12; Luke 23:46 with Psalm 31:1-5.
127. Acts 2:23
128. "In the language of Scripture, something foreknown is not simply that which God was aware of prior to a certain point. Rather, it is presented as that which God gave prior consent to, that which received His favorable or special recognition. Hence, this term is reserved for those matters which God favorably, deliberately and freely chose and ordained' (Spiros Zodhiates, *The Complete Word Study Dictionary: New Testament* (Chattanooga, TN: AMG Publishers, 2000)).
129. Acts 2:27-28
130. This is the idea behind Francis Chan's book, *Forgotten God*.
131. John 14:1-7
132. John 16:5-15
133. John Macarthur, *Galatians* (Chicago, IL: Moody Press, 1987).
134. I am indebted to Linda Dillow for this discovery. She references 'what if' and 'if only' in her book *Calm my Anxious Heart*.
135. 2 Corinthians 5:17

136. Jonah 3:1

137. W.E. Vine, *Vine's Expository Dictionary of New Testament Words* (Mclean, VA: Macdonald Publishing, 1989).

138. 1 Peter 1:18-19, NKJV

139. The idea for this definition came from Wayne Grudem.

140. Exodus 13:17

141. See Wayne Grudem's *Systematic Theology* (page 321) for an explanation of the will of God/will of man tension.

142. *Dead End Desire: biblical strategies for overcoming self-pity*, 52.

143. R. L. Harris, G. L. Archer, Jr. & B. K. Waltke, *Theological Wordbook of the Old Testament* (Chicago, IL: Moody Press, 1999), 366.

144. Ann Spangler, *Praying the Names of God: A Daily Guide* (Grand Rapids, MI: Zondervan, 2004), 7-8.

145. Elyse Fitzpatrick, *Overcoming Fear, Worry, and Anxiety* (Eugene, OR: Harvest House Publishers), 118-119.

146. The three circles are a modification by Nicholas Ellen on an article by Paul Tripp in which Tripp writes: "Defining responsibilities is also very important. Many counselees are confused about what they are and are not responsible for. . . Most of the people with whom I do this find it helpful. I set it up very simply by saying 'All of us have two circles in our lives, a narrower circle of responsibility and a wider circle of concern. Our circle of responsibility contains all the things God has called us to do. Here we are called to obey. These responsibilities we can give to no one else. They are commands to us in our God-ordained situation. The second circle is the circle of concern. In this circle are things that are important to us and part of our daily concern but that are not our responsibility to produce and are not under our control. These things we must entrust to God I want you to take the things in your life and place them in the proper circle. It also clarifies the cause of anger, anxiety, fear, manipulation, passivity, and many other sins. Attempting to control where you are called to trust and failing to act where you are called to obey are roots of every sort of evil" (Paul Tripp, "Homework and Biblical Counseling, Part2," The Journal of Biblical Counseling: Volume 11, Number 3, Spring 1993 (Glenside, PA: CCEF), 17). Nicholas Ellen introduced the idea of a 3rd circle. He called it "consumed." The more anxious you become about the things you can't control, the more you move away from the things God holds you responsible to control.

About the Author

Phil Moser is the author of the Biblical Strategies Series. He is a pastor, blogger (philmoser.com) and conference speaker. He holds a degree in Business Management, and earned his Masters of Divinity from The Master's Seminary. He presently serves as the teaching pastor of Fellowship Bible Church in Mullica Hill, New Jersey. He has served as an adjunct professor teaching the Bible, theology, apologetics, homiletics, and counseling in Albania, Korea, Germany, Hungary and Ukraine. He has been happily married to his wife Kym for over 25 years, and they have four children.

About Biblical Strategies

Biblical Strategies exists to provide resources for those who desire to change, but need help taking the next steps.

- The series is comprised of brief booklets that explain and apply Biblical passages to a specific struggle.
- The accountability plan helps the reader overcome the temptation by implementing the key growth habits of prayer, scripture memory, daily Bible readings, and application of truth.
- The Scripture Retrieval System is a memory aid in which Biblical passages have been selected for each temptation. Ten of the passages expose temptation's deception; the remainder weaken temptation's appeal as truths about the character of God and the nature of the gospel are committed to memory.

Biblical Strategies
How you get to where God's taking you.
BiblicalStrategies.com